Radical

SKIING

Paul Mason

Heinemann
LIBRARY

H www.heinemann/library.co.uk
Visit our website to find out more information about Heinemann Library books.

To order:
☎ Phone 44 (0) 1865 888066
📄 Send a fax to 44 (0) 1865 314091
💻 Visit the Heinemann Library Bookshop at www.heinemann/library.co.uk to browse our
catalogue and order online.

First published in Great Britain by Heinemann Library,
Halley Court, Jordan Hill, Oxford OX2 8EJ,
a division of Reed Educational and Professional Publishing Ltd.
Heinemann is a registered trademark of Reed Educational & Professional Publishing Limited.

OXFORD   MELBOURNE   AUCKLAND
JOHANNESBURG   BLANTYRE   GABORONE
IBADAN   PORTSMOUTH NH (USA)   CHICAGO

© Reed Educational and Professional Publishing Ltd 2002
The moral right of the proprietor has been asserted.

Designed by Celia Floyd
Illustrated by Jeff Edwards
Originated by Universal
Printed in Hong Kong by Wing King Tong

ISBN 0 431 03693 4
06 05 04 03 02
10 9 8 7 6 5 4 3 2 1

British Library Cataloguing in Publication Data

Mason. Paul
Skiing. – (Radical sports)
1. Skis and skiing – Juvenile literature
I. Title
796.9'3

Acknowledgements

The Publishers would like to thank the following for permission to reproduce photographs: Action plus: 18a; Allsport:
25, 26, 27; Corbis: 24; Images: 29; John Cleare: 18b, 18c; John Noble: 22; Mary Evans Picture Library: 4, 5; O Robson -
Stock Shot: 6, 7a, 7b, 8, 9a, 9b, 9c, 10a, 10b, 11, 12a, 12b, 13a, 13b, 13c, 13d, 14a, 14b, 14c, 15a, 15b, 15c, 16, 17a,
17b, 17c, 17d, 20a, 20b, 21; Skishoot-offshoot: 23.

Cover photograph reproduced with permission of FPG.

Our thanks to Jane Bingham for her help in the preparation of this book.

Every effort has been made to contact copyright holders of any material reproduced in this book. Any omissions will be
rectified in subsequent printings if notice is given to the Publisher.

This book aims to cover all the essential techniques of this radical sport but it is
important when learning a new sport to get expert tuition and to follow any
manufacturers' instructions.

CONTENTS

INTRODUCTION

A short history

People have been skiing for over 4000 years! At least that long ago, people in Norway and Sweden were crossing snowy landscapes on long wooden skis. Skiing continued to be just a way of travelling around until the mid-nineteenth century when people suddenly discovered that skiing was great fun!

In the European Alps, people started strapping skis to their feet and sliding down the mountainsides. At about the same time, Norwegian **immigrants** brought skiing to the USA. People loved the feeling of speed as they whizzed downhill through the snow.

Another invention was needed before skiing could become really popular – the tow rope. Tow ropes dragged skiers back to the top of the slope without effort. People could learn to ski quickly because it took less time to get to the top of the slope, leaving more time for skiing back down again.

Early skiers didn't have special clothes. Men wore suits and coats, and women wore big skirts.

This old photograph shows tourists enjoying a day out in the mountains in Switzerland in about 1900. They are using a rope to help them climb the mountain.

Skiing today

Today there are thousands of ski **resorts** all round the world and many different ways of having fun on their slopes. Skiers can choose downhill skiing, **snowblading**, cross-country or **free-heel skiing**.

THE SECRET LANGUAGE OF SKIING

These are some of the words skiers use that you might not have heard before:

Binding the device that attaches the ski to the ski boot.

Carving turning by digging the sides of the ski into the snow, rather than sliding them around.

Edge the metal edge at the side of the ski, which is used to grip the snow during turns.

Free-heel skiing skiing across different terrain, including uphill, using skis that attach to the ski boots only at the toe.

Piste a marked route down the side of a mountain for skiers to follow.

Snowblading a kind of skiing that uses short skis and a slightly different binding (see page 9).

Telemarking another word for free-heel skiing – the name comes from the Norwegian town of Telemark, where this type of skiing was invented.

THE SKIS FOR YOU

Choosing the right skis

The best skis for you depend on your height and weight. It's a good idea to rent equipment at first because you get to know the length and style of ski that suits you best. Once you have decided on a particular type, you can splash out on your own equipment.

Different words describe the various parts of a ski:

Skiers use poles like these to help them balance during turns and to move across flat ground.

Tail

Edges

Edges cut into the snow and allow the ski to grip during turns.

Tip

Different ski schools give different advice to students about the length of ski they should be using. Some start beginners on very short skis, which are easier to control. As they get better, the students move on to longer and longer skis. Other ski schools start beginners on full-length skis.

TOP TIP

On your first ski trip, you will probably rent equipment. Take the advice of the people in the rental shop about what you should be using. If you feel later that different equipment would be better, the shop will let you go back and change your skis or boots.

Traditional skis are great for downhill speed, but not as good for carving turns. They have fairly straight edges, and are among the longest skis. Telemark skis are for **telemarking** (also called '**free-heel skiing**') which combines downhill skiing with cross-country. Telemark skiers can ski up hills as well as down.

Cross-country skis

These skis are used for skiing along flat ground rather than going downhill and are long and thin for speed.

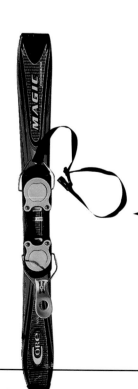

Carvers

Carving skis come in a variety of different lengths. They are shorter than traditional skis and better for carving turns, but don't travel as fast in a straight line. The edges of carving skis curve inwards at the middle, near the boot.

Snowblades

These are shorter than other skis – usually less than 1 metre long. They are easier to control than long skis, and many people find learning on snowblades easier than on longer skis, partly because snowbladers don't use poles.

BOOTS AND BINDINGS

Keep your feet happy!

One of the most important pieces of equipment in skiing is your boots. Uncomfortable boots can make skiing miserable. When your boots cause you pain, it becomes very hard to control your skis, or to think about anything other than how much your feet hurt! If your rented boots start hurting, take them back to the shop and change them for another pair.

TOP TIP

- If your boots turn out to be a little too big, you can wear extra socks to fill them up. These will give your feet a bit of extra padding as well!

CHOOSING BOOTS

Your ski boots need to fit you well without being uncomfortably tight.

- Stand up in your boots with them done up. If your feet feel crushed, you need a larger pair.

- Bend your knees forwards so that your shins are resting on the front of the boot. Are they comfortable?

- Lean back so that your calves are against the back of the boot, to check for comfort.

- Do the same test leaning from side to side.

- After all this, how do your ankles feel? If they are sore, try another pair of boots.

Bindings

The **binding** is the piece of equipment that attaches the ski to the ski boot. There are different bindings for different types of ski.

Release binding

This binding holds the boot on to the ski at the toe and the heel. As the skier steps into it, it clicks shut. To get your boot out of the binding, you push down with your ski pole on a catch at the side, which releases your heel. In a fall, the binding snaps open again. This is to stop the skier's legs getting badly twisted or broken.

Free-heel binding

This type of binding is used for **telemark** and cross-country skiing. It allows the skier to lift their heel away from the top of the ski. Free-heel bindings release in a fall.

Snowblade binding

This binding is simpler than a release binding. It does not release in a fall but, because snowblades are shorter than other skis, there is less risk of injury.

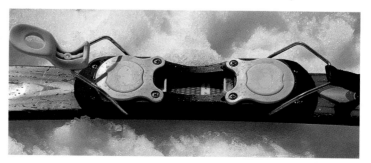

THE RIGHT CLOTHES

It's important to keep warm in the mountains. If you start to get cold, it becomes harder to concentrate and you will be more likely to have an accident.

Some skiers wear a thick, warm jacket with a single layer of clothes underneath, but many people prefer to wear several thinner layers of clothes. That way they can add or take away layers according to the temperature.

Helmet ·····················▶

This is an essential item. If you break an arm or leg it will mend, but if you damage your head you may never recover.

Gloves ·····················▶

These need to be warm and waterproof. The best ones have a removable inner glove, which allows you to dry the glove out quickly.

SAFETY FIRST

Always use sunscreen with a high protection factor in the mountains. Without it your face and lips will burn and then blister very quickly. This is because light reflects from the snow as well as shining directly on to your face.

TOP TIP

Be prepared for the weather to change very fast. You may have set out on a bright sunny day but, by the afternoon, it could be snowing and windy.

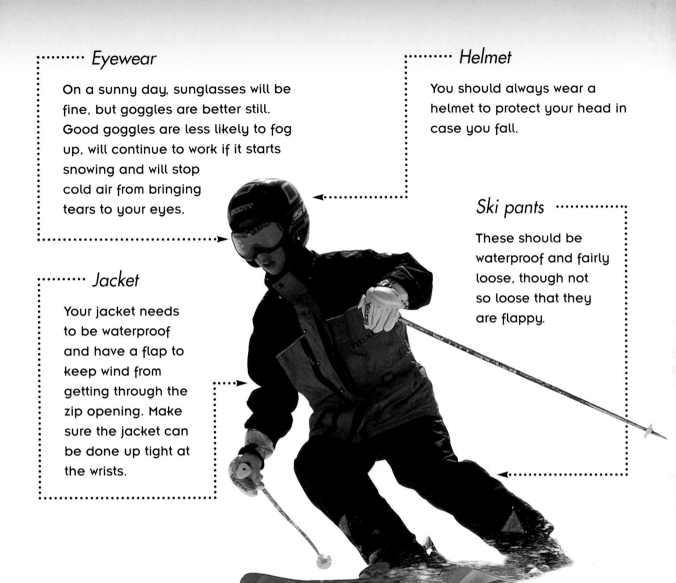

Eyewear

On a sunny day, sunglasses will be fine, but goggles are better still. Good goggles are less likely to fog up, will continue to work if it starts snowing and will stop cold air from bringing tears to your eyes.

Helmet

You should always wear a helmet to protect your head in case you fall.

Ski pants

These should be waterproof and fairly loose, though not so loose that they are flappy.

Jacket

Your jacket needs to be waterproof and have a flap to keep wind from getting through the zip opening. Make sure the jacket can be done up tight at the wrists.

It is a good idea to wear a fleece jacket, especially if your outer jacket doesn't have a warm lining. Try to get one that keeps your neck warm when zipped up. Thermal top and tights are a layer of clothes designed to wear next to your skin. They take moisture away from your body, stopping the dampness from cooling you down and trapping the heat.

Some skiers wear thin socks, but most prefer special, thick ski socks. A few skiers even like them so much that they wear two pairs!

KEEPING FIT AND HEALTHY

Getting fit

It is worth trying to build up a little extra fitness before you go on a skiing trip. If you are tired while skiing it becomes hard to learn new techniques. You are also more likely to have an accident.

Warming up

Spend a few minutes stretching your muscles before you ski. This makes it less likely that you will injure a muscle. It also helps you to start skiing better sooner, as your muscles are already warmed up when you start. When you've finished skiing, do the stretches again. You will find it less painful to leap out of bed the next morning, when you want to go skiing again!

TOP TIP

As you stretch, breathe deeply from your stomach for six or seven breaths, concentrating on relaxing your muscles. Then stop the stretch.

Calf stretch

Bend one knee while keeping the other leg out straight with your heel on the floor and toe pointing upwards. You will feel the muscles in your calf and behind your knee stretch. Repeat with the opposite leg.

Hamstring stretch

Lean in, facing a wall, with your hands or forearms flat against it. One leg should be bent and the other straight. Lean in further by bending your elbows; the muscles in the back of your straight leg will stretch. Repeat with the opposite leg.

Quadricep stretch ···➤

Stand with your feet flat on the floor. Lift one foot up behind you and use both hands to pull it in towards your bottom. You will feel your thigh muscle stretch. Make sure you don't arch your back while doing this stretch; your hips should stay parallel with the floor.

Back stretch ···┐

Kneel on the floor with your toes pointing backwards. Drop your forehead to the floor with your arms stretched out in front of your head.

Arm stretch ····································

Pull your elbow behind your head with your opposite hand, so that your arm is dangling down the line of your spine. Repeat with the other arm.

Neck stretch

Lean your head gently to the left, roll it slowly forwards and then to the right. Do the same thing in reverse. Never bend your neck backwards: this is bad for it.

Eating for skiing

It is important for skiers to eat enough of the right kind of food. Foods with plenty of carbohydrate are good: bread or pasta are ideal. If you also eat food with fat in it – cheese, for example – your stomach takes a long time to break down the fat. Meals with carbohydrate and fat give you a quick burst of energy from the carbohydrate, then a slow burn of back-up energy from the fat.

THE BASIC SKILLS

The snowplough

Almost all skiers begin by learning a technique called the **snowplough**. The technique gets its name from the shape your skis make, with the tips close together and the **tails** far apart.

The snowplough technique allows you to control the speed of your skis and to choose the direction you turn. It looks very different from more advanced skiing, where the tips and tails of the skis are the same distance apart.

Neutral stance

All skiers, whether they are experts or beginners, should aim to have a **neutral stance**. This means that you should not have more weight on one part of your boots than another. In particular, avoid leaning back on your calves because this will make the skis accelerate away from you.

Slowing down

Push the tails of the skis out using your knees and heels. You will start to slow down.

Stopping

As you push the tails still further apart you will come to a stop.

Snowplough turns

Keeping the same amount of weight on each foot will allow you to travel in a straight line. If you think you are going too fast, push the tails of your skis outwards to slow down. If you are going too slow, let the tails come together a little.

To turn to your right, turn your left hip forwards slightly and put extra weight on your left foot.

Your left ski will turn in front of you, bringing the right ski round with it.

To turn back to the left, repeat the process in reverse, starting by putting extra weight on your right foot.

SAFETY FIRST

Pick a gentle slope to start skiing! Each ski **resort** has a special area set aside for beginners, called the nursery slopes. Here, classes meet each morning or afternoon to learn the basics of skiing. These classes are the best way to learn how to ski, with a group of people who are also beginners.

PARALLEL SKIING

Once you have mastered the snowplough, you will want to start skiing with the tips and **tails** of your skis the same distance apart. This is called **parallel skiing**. As with the basic technique, most of the time you should aim to be in a **neutral stance** (see page 14). Your poles will be held loosely under your arms or at your side most of the time but, during turns, you might want to use them for balance.

At first, you will only feel comfortable skiing parallel in a straight line across the slope (this is called **traversing**) and your turns will still be done in the **snowplough position**. The next step is to make your turns in the parallel position as well. When doing parallel turns, your knees should be bent and your shoulders should be in line with your knees. Try not to twist your body.

Start by crossing the slope to the left with your skis parallel. It is best to start practising this on a gentle slope. Ease your weight off the **edges** of your skis. You will start to turn down the slope, into what is known as the **fall line**. Allow your left ski to move ahead of the right ski. You will speed up slightly. As you begin to move into the fall line, put weight on the **inside edge** of both skis. You will start to turn across the fall line.

SAFETY FIRST

 Be aware of the snow conditions when you are learning. Remember it is harder to ski when the snow is frozen and icy.

Continue to put weight on the inside edges of your skis until you have finished your turn.

When you are pointing in the right direction, return to the neutral stance so that you can carry on.

To turn to the left, repeat this process in reverse, allowing your right ski to move ahead of your left as you accelerate into the fall line.

The best way to learn advanced techniques is on a gentle slope. Once you feel confident, move on to a slightly steeper slope. You will suddenly find the technique harder again but, each time you relearn it on a new slope, it will be easier to master.

ON THE SLOPES

When you get to the **resort** you will need to rent skis and boots if you do not have your own. You will also need to get a lift pass. This ticket allows you to use the lift system to travel around the mountains. There are three different types of lift.

Chair lifts

Chair lifts usually carry between two and six people. To catch one you go through the gate and stand in front of the lift. As you sit down, pull the safety bar down in front of you. (Don't forget to push it back up just before getting off!)

Cable cars

Cable cars can fit between four and about forty people and you must take off your skis to travel in them. In smaller ones you sit down, but in larger ones you stand up. (The small ones are sometimes called 'bubbles'.)

Drag lifts

There are two main kinds of drag lift. Button lifts are fitted between your thighs, while T-bars go behind your bottom and are often shared with another skier. Drag lifts have a lot of stretch in them to give you time to get in position before they pull you up the slope. When the light is green, slide slowly through the gate and grab the lift pole. Fit the button or T-bar into a comfortable position, and wait for the lift to start pulling you up the hill. Lean back a little and relax your legs to stop the lift from pulling you off balance.

Piste maps

Piste maps help you to find your way around the resort. They show where the ski runs – called 'pistes' – go, as well as the location of restaurants and first-aid posts. The runs are graded using slightly different colours. Pistes are given a grade according to how difficult they are to get down. If you are a complete beginner, it is best to stick to the easiest runs at first, while you build up your confidence.

SAFETY FIRST

Drag lifts can sometimes be tricky to use, as they may pull quite hard when you first get on. Make sure you are ready to ride the lift. Don't grab the lift pole until you are in position and completely ready. If you have lessons, the instructor will show you how to catch the lifts.

CARING FOR YOUR EQUIPMENT

It is important to look after your skiing equipment for two reasons. First, equipment that has not been looked after is much more likely to break. This could cause you to have a nasty accident. Second, skiing equipment that has been cared for works better.

Looking after your skis

The metal **edges** of your skis need to be sharp or you will find it hard to turn. Take a careful look at them to check whether there are any deep scratches on the edges: if there are, you may need to have them sharpened. If so, take them to a ski shop and have the job done by a professional using a special machine.

The edges of this ski are scratched and blurry, so they need to be sharpened.

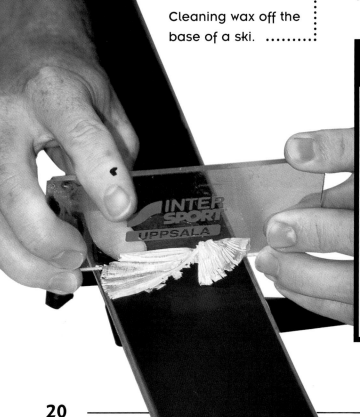

Cleaning wax off the base of a ski.

SAFETY FIRST

Sometimes skiers run over bare earth or rocks, which can gouge a deep chunk out of the bottom of their skis. If this happens, take your skis into the shop as soon as possible. If the gouge has gone through the wax and into the base of the ski, then it will need to be repaired in case water soaks in.

The base of your skis will be covered with wax. The wax makes the skis travel faster. As you ski, this wax is slowly worn away, especially if you accidentally go over stones or earth. Make sure that your skis are waxed regularly (about once for every two to four weeks of use). It is best to have this done by a specialist ski shop.

Checking your bindings and boots

Check your **bindings** each morning before you ski by rocking them forward and back, then from side to side. If there is any movement, something may need to be tightened up or repaired. You also need to check any fastenings on your boots to make sure that nothing has come loose.

TOP TIP

Have your skis waxed before you put them away for the summer. This will stop the edges from rusting.

The bottom of a ski needs to be waxed regularly.

RULES OF THE SLOPES

Collisions between skiers are highly dangerous. Even at slow speeds, it is easy to break a leg or an arm. Several skiers each year are killed when they crash into one another at high speed. To prevent accidents, there are rules all skiers and snowboarders have to follow.

The downhill skier has the right of way

Skiers further down the slope cannot see you coming from behind them. You must make sure you have plenty of room to pass by. If you do not have room, slow down to their speed until there is plenty of space.

Stick to the marked ski runs

Even if you can see that other skiers have left the ski run, do not follow their tracks. They may be far better skiers than you and able to avoid hazards such as rocks, trees and **crevasses**. However, they may just have skied off a cliff around the corner so it is always best to stick to the marked ski runs.

Safety on the ski run is important. It is best to stick to marked ski runs.

Don't stop in obstructive or invisible positions

The middle of a busy ski run is not the best place for a drink stop. Nor is just over the brow of a hill, where other skiers and snowboarders may not be able to see you until it is too late. Always stop at the edge of the ski run.

Keep control of your skis

Runaway skis can do a lot of damage, so make sure they don't slide away as you are putting them on.

Only ride ski runs you can cope with

If you go on a ski run that is too difficult for you, it is far more likely you will have an accident.

Obey special signs

If a ski run is closed, do not go down it. There may be machinery at work, or the risk of an **avalanche**. You will put yourself in danger, as well as the people who have to come and rescue you in an emergency.

Always obey warning signs. They are put there to help you avoid danger.

23

COMPETITIONS

There are several different kinds of skiing competition and most of them have races for every level of ability. Young skiers, inexperienced skiers, skiers with disabilities – these and many others enter ski races of many different kinds. To reach the top in any of the events, skiers have to be very talented and extremely fit. Most of the best racers have been skiing since they were three or four years old!

Racers go downhill through a series of gates, which are marked by coloured poles that guide the skier down the course. The speed at which they can travel is determined by how close together the gates are. Slower races have more gates; faster races have fewer gates.

Slalom

This is the event where the gates are set closest together. Slalom racers have to combine speed with technical skills as they weave their way down the slope.

Giant slalom

Giant slalom is a cross between slalom and downhill. There are more gates than in downhill, but skiers have to make fewer turns than in slalom. There is a variation of giant slalom called super-giant slalom, which is more like downhill.

Competition-standard skiing in the giant slalom.

Downhill

This is the fastest and most dangerous of the ski racing events. The gates are really there only to guide the skiers along the race route. They ski flat out at speeds that can reach over 100km per hour. Even so, there are often only fractions of a second between each place.

Ski jumping

In ski jumping competitions, skiers launch themselves from specially built ramps to see who can travel furthest through the air. Some jumpers can leap over 100 metres before landing.

Cross-country

In cross-country events, skiers race around a course to see who can finish in the fastest time. There is also an event called a biathlon, which combines cross-country racing with target shooting.

Ski-jumping is one of the most spectacular sports to watch.

SKIING GREATS

The world's top ski racers compete in a series of races run by the International Skiing Federation. The most successful racer in each event is crowned World Cup winner at the end of the season. Every four years the skiers get the chance to compete for the ultimate sports prize – an Olympic gold medal.

Every skier on the World Cup Circuit is able to ski extremely fast. Anyone who manages to win even one race has managed a great achievement. Some skiers, though, stand out by being able to win again and again.

Picabo Street

Picabo Street's father once told Jean-Claude Killy, the French downhill Olympic gold medallist, 'I've got a daughter who's going to win an Olympic gold medal some day.'

'Good for her,' Killy replied, 'I hope she does.'

In 1998, at the Nagano Winter Olympics, Street was returning to competition from a knee injury she had suffered a year before and a spectacular crash in Sweden ten days previously. She overcame these problems to win the super-giant slalom gold medal, which was presented to her by… Jean-Claude Killy!

Picabo Street celebrates her gold medal at the 1998 Winter Olympics.

The Herminator – Hermann Maier – shows his powerful technique during a giant slalom race.

'The Herminator'

Hermann Maier, otherwise known as 'The Herminator' because of his aggressive skiing style, is one of the most successful skiers of today. Maier joined the Austrian youth team at the age of fifteen, but was soon dropped because he was too small. He took a job as a bricklayer's apprentice and seven years later the Herminator was big enough to force his way back into the Austrian team. He went on to win an Olympic gold medal at the Nagano Games of 1998.

Franz Klammer

Franz Klammer won 23 World Cup downhill races in his career. In 1976 he was in one of the most exciting events ever at the Winter Olympics in Innsbruck. Coming into the last kilometre of the course he was behind but Klammer skied the last part of the course thrillingly, always seeming as though he was about to crash, and just managed to sneak ahead and claim first place.

Annemarie Moser-Proll

Annemarie Moser-Proll is another legendary Austrian skier, who learnt to ski at the age of four and won the women's World Cup a record six times. In 1973, she won eleven downhill races in a row, a feat that has never been equalled. She also won a gold medal at the 1980 Lake Placid Winter Olympics.

ENDLESS WINTER

It is always winter somewhere around the world. It may be bright sunshine in the Rocky Mountains in June and July, but at the same moment it is cold and snowy in the South American Andes. There is always somewhere you can go skiing.

Some people love skiing so much that they follow the snow around the world. In March they may be working in a **resort** in Colorado, USA, or the European Alps. By July or August they could be in New Zealand or Argentina. Whatever job comes up is fine – ski instructor, lift attendant or washer-up in a restaurant – as long as it leaves time for skiing.

Skiers at Mount Whitcombe in New Zealand.

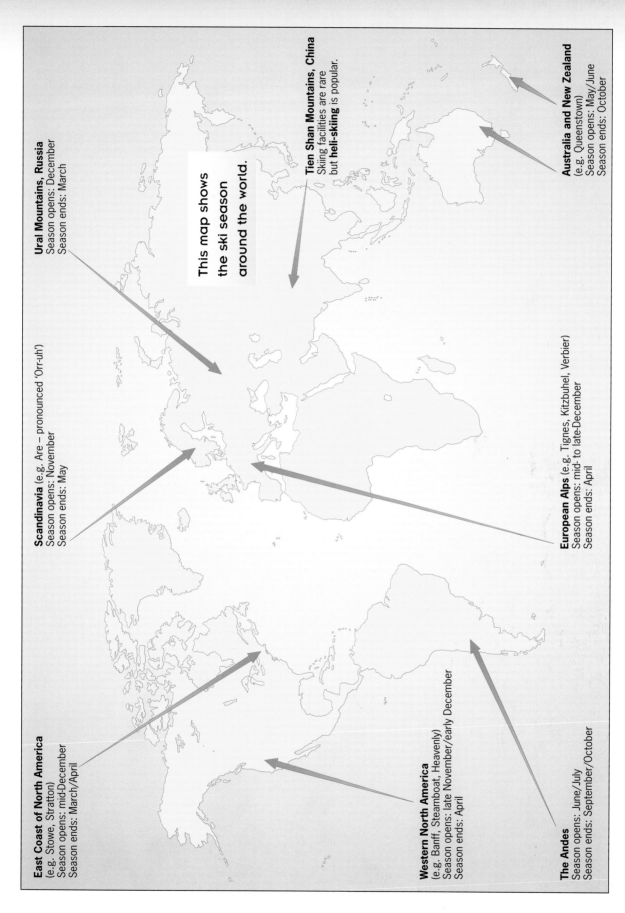

Ural Mountains, Russia
Season opens: December
Season ends: March

Tien Shan Mountains, China
Skiing facilities are rare
but **heli-skiing** is popular.

Australia and New Zealand
(e.g. Queenstown)
Season opens: May/June
Season ends: October

This map shows
the ski season
around the world.

Scandinavia (e.g. Are – pronounced 'Orr-uh')
Season opens: November
Season ends: May

European Alps (e.g. Tignes, Kitzbuhel, Verbier)
Season opens: mid- to late-December
Season ends: April

East Coast of North America
(e.g. Stowe, Stratton)
Season opens: mid-December
Season ends: March/April

Western North America
(e.g. Banff, Steamboat, Heavenly)
Season opens: late November/early December
Season ends: April

The Andes
Season opens: June/July
Season ends: September/October

GLOSSARY

avalanche   sudden movement of snow down a mountainside

binding   device that attaches your ski boot to your ski

carving   digging the edges of your skis into the snow so they don't slip sideways (when you look back up the hill, a carved turn has left an obvious line showing the route you took)

crevasses   deep cracks in ice or rocks

edge   metal strip that runs down each side of a ski (the edges allow skis to grip the snow during turns)

fall line   direction in which a stone would travel if you rolled it down the slope (usually straight downhill)

free-heel skiing   type of skiing using a binding that attaches the ski to the boot only at the toe

heli-skiing   where skiers are dropped off at the top of an empty slope by helicopter

hypothermia   condition of having an unusually low body temperature (although people can recover from mild hypothermia, it is also possible to die from severe hypothermia)

immigrants   people who come from somewhere else to live in a new country

inside edge   the edge of the ski that points towards the top of the slope or the inside of a turn

neutral stance   basic position for all skiers, in which you stand evenly on your skis without putting extra weight on any part of your boots or skis

parallel skiing   technique where you ski with the tips and tails of your skis an equal distance apart

piste   marked route down the mountain for skiers

resort   place where people come to ski, and which has lifts, restaurants and other facilities for skiers

snowblading   kind of skiing that uses very short skis and no poles

snowplough position   the position with which most people learn to ski, with the tips of the skis close together and the tails of the skis further apart

tail   back part of the ski

telemarking   another word for free-heel skiing

traversing   skiing across a slope rather than down it

USEFUL ADDRESSES

British Ski and Snowboard Federation
Hillend
Biggar Road
Midlothian, EH10 7EF

The Ski Club of Great Britain
The White House
57–63 Church Road
Wimbledon
London, SW19 5SB

Australia

Skiing Australia
Level 32
525 Collins Street
Melbourne
Vic 3000
Tel: 03 9614 2644
www.skiingaustralia.org.au

FURTHER READING

Books for children

The best places to hunt for children's books about skiing are on the Internet and in libraries. Few books on skiing have been published recently, but some libraries may have:

Skiing On The Edge, Bob Italia (Abdo and Daughters, 1993)

All Action Skiing, Michelle Steinburg (Wayland, 1993)

Other books

Skiing for Dummies, Allen St John (IDG Books, 1999)

Skiing and the Art of Carving, Ellen Post Foster (Turning Point Ski Foundation, 1997)

From Tip To Tail: Basic Alpine Ski Tuning, D.J. Rader (Cornerstone, 1996)

Magazines

There are no ski magazines specifically for children, but two good magazine publications are:

Fall Line
A general magazine with information on resorts, techniques, equipment and other ski-related articles.

The Daily Mail Ski & Snowboard Magazine
This gives advice on all aspects of skiing.

Websites

www.gbjuniorski.com
A website for the British children's ski team.

www.ifyouski.com/bssf/home
The site of the national ski and snowboard federation of Great Britain: a competition-oriented site with links to local ski clubs.

www.fis-ski.com
The site of the organization in charge of the skiing World Cup, with features on racers, news articles, information on different kinds of skiing and links to national organizations.

www.skiclub.co.uk
Website of the Ski Club of Great Britain. Carries information on skiing, resorts, weather and snowfalls, and fitness for skiing.

All the Internet addresses (URLs) given in this book were valid at the time of going to press. However, due to the dynamic nature of the Internet, some addresses may have changed, or sites may have ceased to exist since publication. While the author and publishers regret any inconvenience this may cause readers, no responsibility for any such changes can be accepted by either the author or the publishers.

INDEX

Titles in the *Radical Sports* series include:

Hardback   0 431 03695 0

Hardback   0 431 03690 X

Hardback   0 431 03692 6

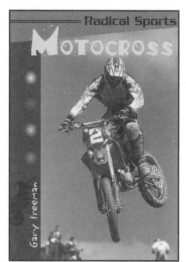

Hardback   0 431 03691 8

Hardback   0 431 03694 2

Hardback   0 431 03693 4

Find out about the other titles in this series on our website www.heinemann.co.uk/library